Free Verse Editions
Edited by Jon Thompson

pH of Au

Vanessa Couto Johnson

Parlor Press
Anderson, South Carolina
www.parlorpress.com

Parlor Press LLC, Anderson, South Carolina, 29621

© 2023 by Parlor Press
All rights reserved.
Printed in the United States of America
S A N: 2 5 4 - 8 8 7 9

Library of Congress Cataloging-in-Publication Data on File

978-1-64317-381-8 (paperback)
978-1-64317-382-5 (pdf)
978-1-64317-383-2 (ePub)

1 2 3 4 5

Front cover photo by Simon Lee on Unsplash. Used by permission.
Back cover photo by Tadeu Jnr on Unsplash. Used by permission
Book design by David Blakesley.

Parlor Press, LLC is an independent publisher of scholarly and trade titles
in print and multimedia formats. This book is available in paperback and
ebook formats from Parlor Press on the World Wide Web at https://www.
parlorpress.com or through online and brick-and-mortar bookstores. For
submission information or to find out about Parlor Press publications,
write to Parlor Press, 3015 Brackenberry Drive, Anderson, South
Carolina, 29621, or email editor@parlorpress.com.

Contents

Contents

See the heartwood's gleam, "brasil" itself an archaic colored-ember-relate, brazilin and brazilein for medieval reddish dye, brasyle in recipe. . . . Heal and flourish.

{Chrysocyon}

1

No drowning

At Versailles, I photographed the cracks
on the floor. Other eyes

toward gold. Marble flowers without
water. Echo of

mirrors. Versailles is too loud.

In the silent

wood-floor room in Brasil,
I eventually

hear: garbage
truck engine, always at 3 a.m.

What we refuse
is taken in the night. But I fear

standing at the bathroom mirror then:

legs

of a cockroach tap-whisper a ripple.

All night long
I don't cup my hands with water.

Brasil & broil

August 2019

There is nothing like being a continent

away from my scorching motherland.

|

Almost a year ago flames took
Museu Nacional in Rio de Janeiro,

over two centuries of artifact
gathering gone. A firefighter's hands

burned in want to save Luzia's bones,
11,500 years beloved, skull with luck

to be found later in fragment. Oh ancestor—
if you could see how much human failure

hurts all these days.

|

Sou uma filha da Amazônia.

I am a daughter of the Amazon.

I've seen the Encontro das Águas,
grown on her fish and fruit for many
summers. And now a river with fire

among it more than ever. Season of the burning.

Century. Era. Of logger and farm

in nation named for a tree.

|

To tweak from Lorca: Amazônia que se quero verde.

The norm of the modern is somnambulism. Our curse
to know the problem and share and
little seem doable.

In this case, don't light a candle.

There are few prayers I really believe in.

The swiftness of amphibians finding damp.

|

I want a prayer of fruits: uma Oração das Frutas

açaí   mamão   abacate

       abacaxí   cupuaçu   goiaba

guaraná   tucumá   graviola

       maracujá   acerola   maça de cajú

I want a prayer of fruits   I may never eat again.

Near Igreja de São Domingos, Lisbon

While sitting, I get

octopus legs in a cold salad

that you don't want to see.
Cubed pearl onions. Someone

bearded and smoking draws

a cathedral where in 1506

one said he saw Christ's face and
another said it was a flame's

reflection on a crucifix; the latter

man taken and burnt in the square.

Yesterday, the tour guide took
us feet away to Ginjinha, spiced

cherry red liquor, which we drink

tomorrow again in another town,

inside a chocolate cup I set
whole in my mouth.

The photoreconnaissance wants an autogiro

at Palácio Nacional de Sintra

We enter a palace room for a second

time, the one where stags hold
some of my ancestors' names.

So many mouths, some little flies.

Camera catch the pitch of my smug.
You try not to spout. My wet crest.

The stags on a ceiling of gilded pens.

So a lens under my chin makes a wish,
I a push. A ropeless turn of my head

leads to an Atlantic edge. Westernmost

point of low return. Never crease the will,
and wander. There's a weigh, out

to the wrong side of a hide but delicious.

I want one pound of not marbled. The artist
scales your face to an itch at the ear.

The phenetics want an autograph

Bromide's touch to a pillar of. Fool's.

Rub the epsom along the water's belly.
Shake a surface into cellulite and eclipse.

Mind us into light's parts. Pilot covered.

Gray water the plants until smoothed.
Leave the cockroach cupped for hours.

My daze is not or numbered. Penciled.

Mouth's glass waits at the juice of plastic.
The wrong soap drunk by machine driven.

Your host is at the point of past refund.

Seldom is the herd of courage yeti-met.
Pink be the salts on the Lazy Susan.

Squash the verb, vegetable. Forehand.

My back to acids and basics, hurts.
Philharmonic phoning phials and treble.

Ear to the ground pepper does little, here.

Considering the Amazon in the Texas Hill Country

Lily pads freckle a creek
beyond the porch. Within,

I push plastic and film
so we watch me prepuberty
on the Amazon. My mother,
grandmother and other

Brazilians where two
rivers of different temperatures
take miles to mix, but they do.
A sloth is not innocent, pinching

me below the thumb.
Does it squeeze? I ask
before the macaw stands on
my hand. This film has

been deteriorating. The sky
is an incorrect pink. It ends.

My current body holds
you and we measure reciprocally.

Mingling of units. Centigrade:
the coolness of toes does not speak
for the whole. Foot: you suggest bareness
outside if I want to toughen up.

Kilogram: I lift you because you doubted
me. You curl eggplant into
an oven in celebration of me. I eat. Always you are
surprised where I manage to put things.

Against your chest, I see your back
on the mirror behind us.

Comfort

I tell the other people at the table
that I am eating goat testicles

and I believe it. I read later: maybe
it's just a mix of tripe.

I show your father my watch with
water droplets in its face. "We swam

yesterday." Eighty percent was me
sitting submerged, you coaxing

out what little potential energy I had.
Self at rest, I said, "I like to cuddle

the water." I let my palms clap
lightly against the surface tension

until you promised that I could float
with little effort. So aerobic.

I prefer the barbell over a bicycle.
When I was seven, I was trying

without training wheels six feet
at a time. My father, annoyed,

got on my tasseled rig and showed
it can be done. Why do you care

what I am doing? What's wrong
with me sitting? I pull close

to a table to do what I see no
one else doing, and I put cheese on it.

gilded or gelid

My mother and I walk into a butcher's shop.

Exit with beef bones for hourfuls

on simmer. My initial use of gifted crock

pot. Elsewhere, gulls above sea level,
but one considers chicken. Approaches
waste vat of chicken tikka masala

and is fool to dive. Is orange until
humans remove the orange. See (no) cur,
hear (no) curr, taste (no) curry.

Out of this week's beef stock
that has been breakfast, I am

before a still frozen chicken this afternoon.

This won't be the first time

I am stopped by a temperature.

Render billow

1.

Follow the mentor across a street,
a jaywalk to rare steak and talk of pepper.

Crosswalk denied again upon return.
My hesitation about headlights,
but mentor goes. I do. Other side.

Then we hear a crack. Car halt.
Follow the curious family to
see the raised head of lying buck.

A teen parks his moped and embraces
the buck into standing. (A risk
taken with panicked tines. I feared.)

The deer, mouth dripping large
red strings, walks towards us,
startles and falls. A mother says,

"No, baby. It's okay. You have to go
that way." We primates.

My passenger later says, "I'm sure
he'll be okay." I say "internal injuries"
and don't properly brake for a speed bump.

2.

My grandfather mumbles in Portuguese
and every seventh word becomes
blood in his mouth.

A two-day bloat from intestinal tumor
pressures his lungs and esophagus.

I tell him to spit in the bag. Try to
act normally as his words turn red.

My imperfect Portuguese
presses against the ceiling.

We do not say that we do
not know if he will live.

My mother, needing something
to say, repeats to the nurse
that his dentures are out.

3.

He is opened while everyone
in a house is wearing red.

I wait as a team loses.

My grandfather lives.

I am offered and eat my first corned beef.

The mentor listens at the driveway.

4.

His colon will lead

to a bag for a while.
It leaks and infects.
Vacuum assisted

wound closure.

My mother siphons
English into something
to which he can nod.

5.

I forget the word for pillow.

What do you call this thing,
I ask. He keeps his eyes closed
and just says, ask correctly.

So I ask him to open his eyes.

6.

After I close my trunk,
I see a doe cross

the street toward me. (At this
house, we feed them sometimes.)

This is guilt. I walk to the patio
and look back at her

until my knee hits rocking chair.

My human skin colors instantly.
The doe safely noses the lawn.

Two more months of lease

The bag of crickets rests

on the island

of the kitchen until after midnight

when you empty

it into a terrarium. I don't
know where I'm going either.

I receive a bowl from your father

emptied of
guac as joke

but I still spoon together specks

of green. Maybe I should
forget how quickly a house sells

or the shore moving in-

land.... No. At the end of each presentation,

at least three different students
say, *And that's all I got.*

A shrug with notecards layered by applause.

Arrive to the smell of roasted

floorboard. The heat

lamp off but left on floor,

a deep hole bloomed
in laminated wood.

White and orange pulp,
twisting crisp edges

that miscommunicating

repairmen can't fix.
What else do you do

in the nights in which I can't stay

up later than you but you have
to rise early? Dawns of bent knees

covered, unsure if you're yet
on your half until simultaneity

is a syzygy near alien on a planet
that grows and shrinks overnight.

It's time for enthalpy to read her horoscope.

I build the evening as [see, saw]

I find my first

white eyebrow hair

within a week post-birthday.

A pizza place's restroom mirrors
with diva dressing
room style lighting made the reveal.

Its length suggests it's
been there a while,

longer than the bagel
half you left
in the toaster and Philadelphia

cream cheese unlidded.
Six hours later I will see
these items with a gasp—

three hours earlier
you laugh at lyrics
I mishear as *scream seasick*

(it was *'scream' she said*).
But the better rhyme and metaphor
has *seasick*. You say your father would fall

out of his chair at this. I remind

you love is a churning

behind the eyes.

Lane

Soon, I'll be alone with the town
you were born in.

The two-lane highway
outside our bedroom had its dividing
line repainted a couple months ago.

The clarity of that yellow appropriate for spring,
but my head turns gray three nights a week since.

I'll replant myself further into town,
where the grid can help repattern me

before you are east for months.
Every other

night, you ask if this will or will
not be goodness; it cannot
be tasted yet.

Pages of wrinkled calculus / I suggested for the sun

I tell him to not leave
the textbook outside
overnight because of dew.

$$\int$$

Earlier: he went in the rain
to find his car among uphill pooling,

and now the math books
he teaches from and a tabletop
roleplaying game book are saturated.

He turns every page. Leaflets veined.

$$\delta$$

At my advice, he sets the textbook on the porch,
a numbered animal belly up.

$$\fff$$

A wet-dry vac slinks into our garage
after a visit to Lowe's—as his

car carpet is still wet four
days later—with the vac overpriced

at the register. Of course its cord is three
feet long. Of course another something

must make up for our imprecision,

say a fifty-foot extension sort.

cervids

I am dead   I say   meaning *weary.*   He wants me

to stop that metaphor.   I put it in the ground

   and my wreathed mouth says

   you want me to outlive you? Oh leave me alone he right

-fully says and enters a hallway.   Then back. In Norway

323 deer went   at the same

time: a lightning storm on a plateau. Bodies

sprinkle a slope   to whose taste. Earth

  water and current yesterday. He returns and I let my ears

    cup clouds that   gather after   steps stop.

{Hylozoism}

materia prima

Anima mundi walks into a bar
and says, I'm already here.

Yliaster can have no alibi
and takes the blame, the cuffs.

Do you even lift, they said.
Philosopher's toned, we said.

Water is not compressible.
Fluid among a crown, ahead

an eighth wander of the world
arrives.

Modern alchemist's autocomplete

Gold is money

Gold island

Gold isotopes

Gold is best

Gold is not enough

Gold is worth

a.
Gold is a pet rock
Gold is a compound or element
Gold is a bad investment
Gold is an element

b.
Gold is best
Gold is bad investment
Gold is back in style
Gold is best gif

c.
Gold is crashing
Gold is cheap
Gold is cold and heavy
Gold is commodity

d.
Gold is dead
Gold is doomed
Gold is down
Gold is dropping

e.

Gold is edible
Gold is elo hell
Gold is everywhere
Gold is easier than silver

f.
Gold is for the mistress
Gold is falling
Gold is from space
Gold is found in what type of rock

g.
Gold is going up
Gold is going to crash
Gold is going to explode
Gold is going to skyrocket

h.
Gold is how much per gram
Gold is how much heavier than water
Gold is heavy
Gold is heavier than silver

i.
Gold is inert
Gold is it real
Gold is it a good investment
Gold is indestructible

j.
Gold is just a windy kansas wheatfield

k.
Gold is kitchen
Gold is king

l.
Gold is low
Gold is like a pet rock

Gold is losing its luster
Gold is losing its value

m.
Gold is money
Gold is more active than copper
Gold is money 2
Gold is made of

n.
Gold is not enough
Gold is not a compound
Gold is not an investment
Gold is not a good investment

o.
Gold is opaque and reflective. it has a
Gold is only going to get worse
Gold is over
Gold is on the rise

p.
Gold is pet rock
Gold is power latin
Gold is power
Gold is power artemis fowl

q.
Gold is quote

r.
Gold is real money
Gold is refined by fire bible verse
Gold is real
Gold is red

s.
Gold is soft
Gold is sold by what weights

Gold is space chocolate
Gold is selling for how much per ounce

t.
Gold is the money of kings
Gold is the new pink
Gold is the new black
Gold is the new green

u.
Gold is up
Gold is used for
Gold is undervalued
Gold is up today

v.
Gold is valuable because
Gold is valuable
Gold is more valuable than platinum

w.
Gold is worth
Gold is worthless
Gold is weighed in
Gold is where you find it

x.
why gold is xau

y.
Gold is your trade if you
Gold is yellow

z.
Gold zebra
Gold zipper
Gold zakat calculator
Gold zone

Noli turbare circulos meos*

Take a bath while hearing Kraftwerk.

I've been closer to the autobahn,
then had a gold star mailed back to me.

I forgot it, a gift from someone called aunt.

The whole time Brazilian grandparents
bought me things of that metal

I preferred silver silently. Some white

gold hybrid in a V for my neck. Tiny
diamond eyes unblink. I now know

silver gets dirty. I intentionally

touch and lift iron and check
my body for density.

Do not disturb my circles.

The gold waits in a tin.

* likely (not) Archimedes's last words

Ostomachion

November 2015

Ouro Preto, wait for me.

Rio Doce, cutting the land jagged, you have turned
an unnatural caramel. The dam burst iron ore inside you.

Red not for taste. Kilometers of ecosystem dead.

The fish float like empty gold plates.

Arsenic, mercury, Minas Gerais, amém.

Sweet river, how long will it be.
We sit at a table and look at puzzle pieces we cannot eat.

Spit

Alkahest chuckles.

The universal solvent cannot wear a hat.

So it won't go out…or is out,
we are already dissolved, fooled we're not

homogenous piecemeal. How weird we are still
hungry.

Aqua regia is a saliva to gold. Noble in acid.
Chloroaurate anions pilgrimage, fast.

Alkahest won't flirt. Alkahest doesn't need to flirt.
Alkahest has enough aqua vitae, says, Hi Ethan[ol].

Our slobbery host says, Hold this please, some oil of vitriol.

The roast begins, but the spat is worn.

Digger gold

Ouroboros ought to be a palindrome. Dragon [auto]fell/ate.

Serpent is as serpent does. Until incomplete circuit.

The dead computer's dust on gold wire in the dark
brought out to light. There now, recover.

Continue being for humans. 50% glitter, 40% in pockets,
10% as mechanism. Your worst decade is your acid test.

Asteroid-delivered, the nuggets are not fresh. Don't drink

from the sluice box. Panning out. Kekulé dreamt

of carbon atoms as the eternal reptile, benzene's jaw tight.

Rocking the golden baby

Rocker box fed by hand. The elixir downpour.
The weather is young today. Fountain range

before us. Trommel and the marble track.

Play with plush Hermetic seal, waterproof.
Hungry? Don't have bowl of hygieia.

Pharmaceutic apotheosis's upchuck and colic.

Colostrum in an apothecary jar. Startle or stir
with Rod of Asclepius. If it were caduceus

they would have bit or wingbeat me.

Once, twice, Trismegistus as lady. Do feed
the scrolls. George Berkeley toasting

tar water. Cupboard nostrums politely

or no. This time my season will not change.
One's oxymoron is another's syncretism.

The amalgam nursery holds into the next Age.

Supernumerary

A third [invention of the] wheel.

Not Pollyanna but polycephaly.

The amphisbaena walks in and looks
you in the eye four times. It minds twice.

One animal with two heads or two
animals that share a body. If there is

a head at each end it should be
called a head at each beginning.

Simultaneously forwards and backwards.
An atomic number glistens at seventy-nine.

Sad history's horde unlocks the chest
of a body where it believes gold is.

The chests pile. The elevator closes.

Several ones of me want to go ways.

filius philosophorum

You insinuate belief in the panacea

by scorning the vitamin variety
I double to you. Swallow anyway.

The dishes I do not want

in the sink are miasma to you.
My germ theory: compounded

flatware are more difficult to clean.

Standing water. Eggs open. New
to Brazil, Zika fever might be keeping

small the heads of the gestating.

When—if—born, has microcephaly.
Two-thousand-four-hundred in 2015.

The world: worse than imperfect; thus,

no homunculi for me. My Cartesian
Theater has no playbills/playpens.

But I'd take René's diver, toy to

show buoyancy: use it as paperweight.

Rush

Borba Gato hiding in the green.

Did he kill a fidalgo? Rio das Mortes with mouth open.

Rio das Velhas, he walks by; alluvial glimmer in the shallows.

Silence and the trees and the rivers and the gold for nearly two decades.

Then gold and the noise.

People went
missing from

the coastal towns and fields
because they wanted to find deposits.

The artisans: gone. Essential
services inflated.

Sailors: abandoned harborfuls of ships.

Soldiers: absent from posts.

Priests, friars: deserted spiritual
calling. These luster needs.

Provisions: unhad, such was haste.

The ground where they wanted to look
slowly took them in.

Rush continued

The mbóaba, bipedal, feets in.

Flightless. A civil war in the mining
camps. An immigrant is an emigrant

is an immigrant. A generation of equation
shifts letters sometimes.

Emboabas pressing their trousers
between the brush.

Certainty not in the sertão. Rumors
of gold nugget instead of lead pellet

in muskets in a district with strike.

Most of the ground's gold found
within the first two feet.

quinto de ouro

The 18th century: beings of colonial mind
among those bodies, taxed across the way.

Find. Then you were expected.

Give 20 out of 100. That's what
their golden ratio was. Portugal

gesturing at Brasil, palm up for
the quota. No model can pose

that much. 1:5. An order: all gold
into bars. Some smiles and shakes

of the head into mugs, but the chuckles
kept bottled. Armies there just to check

rules and gold follow each other, no matter

how dark or deep the [sense of] mine.

Meridiano de Tordesilhas

Let t be a vertical line.
Pope draws this line in 1493.

Let João II be frowning,
Isabella I and Fernando II listen.
Papal rep nods. 1494 and t more western.

Let t mean nothing
from 1580-1640. A few Filipe
of all Iberia. Until João o Restaurador.

Let's face it: t not really meaning much.
Gold and other goods as a border becomes
more and more a jagged west.

Sepé Tiaraju, 1756

That pain of others
deciding what a border
be and do; their
sign to unhome home.

Reductions. Reductions. Reductions.

Co ivi oguerecó iara.*

Explode against their Treaty of Madrid
that the land not mine.

Caiboaté not in my eyes.

* "This land has owners" in Guarani.

Libertas Quae Sera Tamen

Joaquim José da Silva Xavier
without formal education but still
cattle driver, miner, and dentist.

It's the late 1780s. Independence
over there. And there. But not Brazil.
And still taxes yet mine production in decline.
So he thinks of Rousseau and revolutions.

The Inconfidência Mineira wants
its own republic. A white flag

with a green triangle with

words on each side

meaning Freedom, Even

If It Be Late. The revolt
planned, but a betrayer:
an exchange for waiving of taxes.
The rebel arrested. Three-year trial.
He assumes responsibility. Ten lives
saved from the death sentence.

They call him Tiradentes. Teeth puller.

They write a document with his blood.

His head and other pieces in city and city and city,

in a colony that becomes a country
with his martyrdom as holiday.

Those two certainties of life pull close to each other before a view.

solanum lycocarpum

I am for the long
-legged and alone

spraying pyrazine in the bush
that would pause others.
Aguaraçu,* you don't know
which bisavós gave you that mane

you shoulder. Something of a mono-
chasial, helicoid cyme myself. Fang me
open for over half your meals. I remain

green even when ripened,
always in season. Land me
as lobeira, a hunger without time
to read my seeds in golden innards.

* or Chrysocyon brachyurus

wildcat mining

The animal who only wants

gold are some humans.

Some mines claw into
the earth without checkmarks.

Sometimes earth
on top of people.

Hazards tail such happenings.

Sometimes the course
of rivers changes before the mouth.

May 2016 in Peru's portion near Brazil,
mercury becomes an acknowledged
citizen of the water. Thus of fish and people.

If gold has elbows, people will take
it by the crook of an arm

until the pit releases something. Then

if metal inhales, we enter its lungs.

Gold salts

First gold cyanide for tuberculosis. Then this.

Misnomer of ionic, injected to ache
or oral (which is less
effective).

Rheumatoid arthritis with a parenteral spice.

The skin may color between
mauve to blue.

Chrysiasis
holding the dermis
without treat or reverse.

Tasteless gold,
leafy gold float and swivel

to an exterior and stay alloy, stay. Pull pants

and see how today's joints are doing.

logarithm and blues

Potenz / kissed / puissance

      -hydronium ion,
your activity is herewith
on record-

pondus hydrogenii

      1909

potentia hydrogenii

if q looked into a mirror

pA pB pC pD pE pF pG

litmus an alphabet

      at 14, the bluest

coded the strong and weak

our hands wander from titrations

rinse with the well-known 7
      and drink

meet your first amphoteric
see how it pets either side

zwitterions by zwitterions

get rigid with tautomerism

aromatic getaway
      not gotten

into the ether/ore

{Kintsugi}

epipromethion

Inside of a whole town
that is without him,

I find the night pecking
my liver. I make a cliff
out of student papers

and try to keep sleeping as if the body

were near. I was this way even before he left,

how the calendar ahead became painted with surrogates
for our joint life. I'm sure a light I brought him is still

on in his room, inside of a city without me;
he's a student again,

an ember of topology homework growing
from one corner to the next.

unerased

My grandmother asked, "Does it feel like being widowed?"

I walk between stones
of buildings and do my job.

One of my walls has a whiteboard

with a vertical slope of your blue words.
Your voice telephones above miles

of a straight-but-flooded road.

I expect: if I see you on a webcam,
I'll need gold between my growing cracks.

I put on a new brand of lipbalm but think
it'll attract bugs, that I can

only wear this far from home.

steep steps

My grandmother is not a widow, not unless
ex-husbands count somehow.

I sat on her Japanese farmhouse staircase
that she imported back with her,

I a child up on dark wood nearing a ceiling.

Where else would it go? Drawers under
each step retained stacks I couldn't read.

She read me of *La Belle et la Bête*, boar-
head man. Today, I realize most of the meat

I'm eating lately is pork bedded in something.

Rice. Eggs as sunset. Pasture of guacamole.
I revisit the same places that you will see

during the taste of next season.

kin/ken

My grandmother knew absence
those years, how he could be gone

four months at a time on ship:
I didn't even have a phone

at the house. There, another
Japanese sunrise. This month,

her siblings' smiles at one table.
And he, her husband, man I synonym

fully with grandfather, man who can build
outside for hours, weeks—hands

calloused in daylight's vigor—feels
vertigo and floors. In days before,

they had taken a piece of his marrow—
connections made and antibiotics

for weeks. My father and I visit
within the first days. Grandfather looks

to be napping, my father goes
to a toilet, and a nurse asks. *I am his*

granddaughter, I say. *He's been waiting,*
she says. When he turns, I wave to his peripheral

vision, and the smile and hug is strong; he alternates
hands on the handle hanging from above, and I know

he'll be alright. Grandfather asks how you are doing
and what I'm writing about these days. *Kintsugi,*

I begin. *Why would you be thinking*
of that? he asks—shimmer of heal.

unreturned

What kind of day are you having
that my three rings cannot catch you?

I send them out into an evening,
afternoon, and night. In the classroom,

a student censures my pronunciation
of *narcissus*. I repeat until I *don't*

care about flowers or *Greeks*,
I just want Amy Lowell's "Bath"

but it ends up being midnight and I'm still dry.

returned

I wake in prophecy of your call

in a morning I otherwise fill
with sleep then squats.

Your voice weaves closed
a hole in my side. You send

me a photo of a tiger approaching

gently, up to glass. In days

I will see you.

The four-day visit

1.

Can you find where I am

still warm? I pick you
up from the airport

and two months are sandwiched

within our four years—my familiar
stranger feeds me a kiss and I am

old and new at once. My bed

illuminates in recognitions
and a pattern is softly drawn
upon our torsos.

We go to a restaurant with triangle
tessellations, and the ramen
heats across my tongue.

2.

I take you to the cinema,
where we watch humans as non-human
and the rich madman has his soliloquy
among light filtered through water.

3.

I teach people how to argue
on a Friday that makes me

say the antonym of what I mean

in multiples inside one sentence.
My brain too fast for my tired mouth.

4.

I don't want to go to space, personally,

but I design a thought exercise
and five people split

into two tables to answer my questions.

5.

A return to you, and into my vehicle

I bring you to wait for new license.

6.

I wear the gifted
shirt from you

to the delight of our mothers
(yours today, mine tomorrow),

a purple with white speaking in flower.

Thread by thread, we are at
a dinner table with your family

at each corner.

7.

Live action *Beauty
and the Beast* onscreen

with your legs on my lap.

We pause and banter each
character. I speak a Venn
diagram into the air

between us, a circle

for the animated version
veiling this newer film.

A theoretical Belle: *Uh, I liked
you better hairy.*

Yes, please, your legs as they are.

8.

It isn't until the third night

that I realize what they've been

doing outside; I've had my eyes

on you, door eager at my home's side-
walk. Six new bluelight lampposts
dig through my bedroom curtains.

9.

Among my parents' fruits, you
whisper a conspiracy of ice cream

to me. So we leave

early enough to crafted
dairy and dairy-

free. Chia and chai

in my scoop. Your spoon
with a purpose

toward my lips. There
are no accidents in this cold.

10.

A reversal within

a full parking lot
and adjacent to metal

gates is not easy.

You are a series
of hands read in mirrors

and when you sit
there is no time for me
to reveal anything to your palms

as a vehicle noses in

waiting for me to clear

the lane and turn.

The exit has a hill,
steep enough to give
a jolt to the front's

right. Attempts at attention
are what I have left

to collect in these remaining minutes.

11.

I panic into the first yard

of drop-off lane. A wall

of cars on my driver's side,
so you widen the trunk's smile

alone. You come back

to the passenger seat

to lean over my eyes.
A steady love through

my sunglasses. You frame

my mouth with yours,

and you exit a door,
the last of today's series

shared with me.
You forget nothing.

knowledge of cord and ache

Both jokes
told to me

today, I bisect
with the punch line.

Doctor, everywhere
I touch myself hurts - | - The finger is broken.

One of the men throws
in a log, and a goat
jumps into that well - | - They didn't notice
                                   the tether.

I clean a surface with a stanza,
a tender to language's [o]missions.

gestures

In place of physical
affection I am

sent memes and gifs.

I do it too. The bear
eating cake at the table.

This is not perfect.

Something done
toward feeling full.

A hand with a baby
chameleon on each finger.

Golden pheasant

The gif begins with the hen

and then the male's natural
outfit stuns. The feathers

like a helmet on his head.

I imagine you preparing

for the test with an upper-

case sigma ignited in
your lobes, summing

while humming, your food
chilling; wings fast.

Snow stagger in snow-rare space

When the snow arrives
one night after two days
of rain, it is not believed

until I hear one neighbor
speak of this shift to
the other through the wall.

I call you immediately
while watching two puppies
beyond my miniblinds—

snow-snooper me says,
"It's sticking." 436 miles

away, but that snow
also layers on your car

this same night at some
hour unknown to me.

...

I wake into a covered

morning, lock my front door,
and find a limp phallus drawn

on the snow on my windshield.

A smile etched above it
retracts any aggression.

I mistake the arch
of the organ for a rainbow at first

before smoothing it away.

I walk the half
mile to the steaming river.

Finger on button, I digitally freeze
sights of this powdered college town,

walking unplanned miles in cold,
the sun already making crackle
the snow from heights. I hurry to see
and to be able to show you these stills.

...

On campus, feet from a statue
with hand perfect for placed snowball,

"I am two miles from car and home"

I tell your dad, your parents amplified
into angelhood by my need and the encounter.

Your mother drives me back on a parallel road,
not knowing you are emailing us three

photos of your own snow-crusted car and trees.

Key stagger

Two nights before you'd be
back here, I'm outside

my car. Groceries neatly

on floorboard. Keys on
the seat, locked in. Of course,

I said no ice needed for the fish.

"This would be so much easier
if he were here," I say to your

mother on the phone, as you
also have a home key. Property

manager at her child's play. She

can bring the key by after. I decide
it odd to lag next to my vehicle.

I hood my head against the store,

loitering into stiffness, looking to each head-
light. Your parents' angelhood continues:

dad's drive of me to home,

my fetch of spare car
key under couched papers.

brume

These roads are filled with crossing
clouds as I take us to the river.

The rain tessellates
between sky and surface,

our umbrellas an interruption
of unfolded octagons.

I say the name on the list. You get
hot chocolate before we are surrounded

by a percentage of children. Called
to the boat, we sit above glass bottom

with a roof against which the mist whispers.
We smile in murky photos: We've been

on this spring-fed water before, but not
like this, and not together. The next day,

we watch a woman and her love, amphibious,
approach docks in rain on cinema screen.

They think this is goodbye. Your shape is with
me now, me in my teal-sweater-dressed body.

When you are gone again, I will know it is part
of this cycle where we say distance

has no surface tension. My wet sweater
dresses empty of me, drying.

strategy

We both warm soups and sit

before Bond films. We critique
agents and agency. Go through

the checklist: skiing, boating,
casino—

Pause.

I pick ten cards from a stack
and ask you to say the theorem/

formula/expression/proof.
Proud mathematical emblems

with secrets you can specify
by your third try at most.

Again

I say, a cross[-legged] villain
[on the floor, a villain as much

as a Daddy Long Legs is a father].
I nip at an oatmeal cookie waiting

for your answers, piling

them into *Got It* and *Not Yet*. I plan
for your triumph.

sheathing tap

With a hard freeze on the way, outdoor
faucets will need cover. I pick

up your holey red polo that's been waiting
on the floor by the trashcan.

You hold it still as I make cuts
you aren't sure of: you were thinking strips

but I know keeping the sleeve a sleeve
will make easy fitting. Just four

days ago, you were the one wrapping
gifts: I trust your geometry

on those objects, steady scissors.
Right now, I grab three

large rubber bands and go outside
with these red cloths.

I like doing what doesn't need
to be pretty.

counting

I begin measuring my suitcase and considering
if I can live absent
what can't fit in it
for some days.

This mixed potato sack of a decision I unroot
and mash. Colander
hammock. My bed-

half—if I stay, I have all of it again. If I go
with you, there's
a bigger mattress.

I am unsure deep into the morning
when I have coffee
for the first time in

years across from your parents
and beside your edible waffle. Then back
to my place and the load

begins to your car. I decide
a seat is for me and I take it.

driven to ambit

After our longest road
trip, you turn

on your heater that's been
off for weeks. We wait

for 20 degrees to rise.
Your lizard, involuntarily

patient in the terrarium
backseated for the drive,

now pampered with heat lamps.
You realize you have nothing

flannel anymore and the warm
sock's partner is gone. I look

at flights for my return
trip under thick cover.

ad | mire

At the botanic garden, a map
claims there is a swamp

and I am a cynic through yards
of paths until boardwalk

over black water. Green lacing
fractions of surface. You spot

a pie-sized portion of honeycomb
floating. Amber grids waiting to feed

unseen animals. This water thick with mirroring
such that I imagine our time doubled for our duplicates,

whom I do not lean to see. This dark fluid an event horizon.

We cannot stay to learn what lurks. We try a perimeter
path, completing our orbit back toward parked

cars and what looks to be wedding guests

we keep our distance from, nearing signs
naming roots within the ground.

laniary

Semester begins. A student picks
at her molars in the back corner

of the classroom. If that is
okay for the first day,

how many teeth will I find
among homework.

I am not near enough to smell whatever

you're chewing in your own second
week of classes.

I try to watch
if I'm spitting when I talk.

The waiting room

My living room is empty of people
usually. I sit on the couch you left

for me. To pass the time, I lift
weights in this room. Develop

a bench press surpassing my bodyweight.
To fill the space, I let some things be

not put away. I take a number
between one and the days until your return

and divide it into a hot bath
and delayed laundry. And when you are

returned for a segmented time, and there is a quiet,
my foresight makes me see how empty the room

will be again. The moon's blink takes a month. I spool
my eyes back to the present, even if it takes a third of the night.

fork, night

About to turn into home's
parking, I see a gray and white kitten

old enough to eat chunks of something spilled

on my path. I divert. Circle. Parallel elsewhere.
I enter my doorway between cat's glances.

I empathize: its hunger. Solitude. I know this

is something to mention to you, for both aw
factor and survival. No bite left in next morning's drive.

boil advisory

A month of neighborhood
streets gutted

for new water lines. Fluent
machine sounds speaking across the morning

and afternoon, when I am

the new navigator mapping today's detour
avoiding a one-way. Conversations

quietly had, typed out by computer

once home. I consider
calling, but if I do, hearing your voice

from your own body might

foam a mesh within me against
which my speech catches.

Midnight hunger grilling

my heart to rareness. I am the animal
left behind.   Who is friend and who

is not the owl outside. I did not

mean my statements to echolocate
unresponsive   bodies identified

but not identifying: I want to be

the question they find worth answering.
In the box   of light in their hands,

the shadow play we're left
to have   should be real enough.

...

I wake   at noon, gentler,
wise to humans'   way

of doing what   they want.
Rest release need.

Spring break

On the second
day you're here, a red
mug breaks in the sink.

I understand the equation
of soap and your hands.

The mug, with Comic Sans
words about loving cocoa,

wasn't sentimental to me anyway.
Your thumb is, though, and bleeds little.

...

Pouring coffee, I sift the mud
of the French Press. I tap a glass body

on the side of the trash can,
dregs-loosen wish,

but they stick as the glass cracks.
With my detritus focus, I don't

understand the breaking
sounds for several seconds.

...

On my sixth day of having you
this week, I'm weak enough

that the refrigerator door, with
its gentle closing nudge, knocks

out a platter I had in both hands:
the rectangular length divides

into tiny triangles. I get a cut
at my ankle. You sweep as I save

a portion of shardless chicken for the oven.

[rubicund | certainty]

Bangle thicker than my thumb

unwrapped, carvings
as deep as my grandmother's story of buying

this red bracelet decades
ago: among
her first purchases in Japan.

Cinnabar? Or painted? Or

otherwise? Two quiet
dragons approach
each other, a sun
low enough for the slight
bisections of waves.

It settles on my dresser,

intimidates me with its
possible composition.

At a trivia night,
I hear a question
about red lacquer
I can now answer:

{Hg well actually—the merc
hurried ale—}

I whisper *mercury* into the ear
of the scribe I love.

Spring Lake

*at what had been the Aquarena Springs theme park in
decades past; San Marcos, Texas*

When the tour guide screams, you are close

enough to ask him if he is fine. Our flashlights
circle the surface from our kayak seats.

The guide asserts his fineness, fish tossed from
his feet. Another breaks

into thumps on my craft, behind my back.

We see where for decades piglets were thrown
into instinctive swimming. When above

the deepest parts, I feel like I'm on a thin
sheet of turbulent glass. The eels are practicing

their vowels elsewhere tonight, away from the crowd

of nutria in the reeds. You say the first thing you learned
about kayaking was how to flip over and over

to an Irish voice. Each swine would answer
to the same name when the ringing started.

You say a mermaid would surface to bottlefeed

porcine Ralph, hoofing water. The tour guide says
the man who played Tarzan swam to the bottom

to put his mouth at the spring; he was saved from gush.
What nearly drowning was like yesterday is the same

as it is when a clown smokes underwater: unhealthy. As

for nearly drowning in the future, your cousin's great
grandson will choose to be a merman, paying

for a splice to become another one living
in the enlarged ocean. Microplastics between

their teeth, men pregnant as seahorses—whatever

people are left from my generation looking
down through glass bottom boats.

Piranha Plop

A piranha sits

on top of my kitchen cabinet like the Cheshire Cat,
open-mouthed grin as I cook.

He came from my ancestors' waters

into my mother's suitcase, into gift
for her mother-in-law, into gift from

my grandmother back to me.

In college, I showed my teeth
in imitation of his, both our faces to a camera.

I'm not sure where my keychain-size piranha

is now—body crisp and delicate; I may
have chipped off bits of fin when handling.

On a hunch, I open the wooden box with my name

and there it is: as red-bellied as ever, small
mouth open mid-chat. What a language

it would have learned if not dead as a babe.

I cannot hear the riddles of the kitchen piranha
or its recipe suggestions, while I'm sure

my rare steaks would be enjoyed. A movie,

though named *Piranha* (1978), has a plural
amount of rubber puppet fish

and was filmed up the road, a body

of water where I've shone flashlights on gar.
The film has a red herring of Claymation

fish walking on fin feet at the military facility. Sure,

why not: let genetic engineering benefit culinary entertainment,
Chef Pygocentrus Nattereri chuckling as contestants

compete on the new cooking show, *My Meal or I, Meal.*

The piranha judge chomping a loser's dish, then the loser.

Additive

The match unfair, I button

from boxing to cupcake
competition. (Complete opp-

osites, you say.) The contestants drop

their mouths at the ingredient
challenge: crickets. I panic the channel

back and remind you about

this three weeks later looming
over the gray recliner.

We will leave *Dune* (1984) paused on
your parents' TV long after

they've come back from the air.

As the first sandworm makes
its appearance, I set slabs

of cake onto cooling racks that sag.

I write your mother's name in red
once fridged, frosted over-

night. The spice: must. And if I were lost

with my Amazon mother in the desert,
striding arrhythmic? Of course flow:

she'd tear an atom of sand

whisk neutrons, protons, and electrons
into water matter, river cutting the dry.

She can feed a creature for centuries.

She can feed a creature she loves for millennia.
My grandfather, helped down onto sofa bulk,

is going to live forever but he won't know it.

The spice: extends. His tongue over a dissolving
tablet. Of course life: he will still have mitochondria

long after the nanites accidentally invade Madagascar

(a lemur slowly turns its head to show a red laser on the side
—think *Terminator*). The spice: folds. When I raise

my metal hands two hundred years from now before

a villain, I'm sent back to tonight. Of course space:
I'm lucky, lessening it, as you heat

my feet to a safe sleep temperature.

savOrOus

Sparrows'   pathos nearing
our toes.   I   eye   you

at our shared table because hunger is universal.

Seated, we each pinch
the fluff of a kolache

and toss   it to the small   visitors.
This is our   last   hour for months.

"Landslide" from the restaurant speakers boosts our taut attention
to these   seconds. You cast   three crumbs even
when the   birds stop   begging.

They wait in a dry
spot under   a car. Suspicion?   Inattention?

Of the two in your bag, the first
kolache you eat is the sweet one.

Both of mine   are the same: I will   be
a creature of repetition again

while you're   away. Just   as how most
Texans call it a kolache no matter what

is inside: my weeks,   whatever   in
them, encased.

l e v e r a g e s

Bend the month and the second

month between us: a new record of grip
to set on my shelf. How do

my hands look on the projector screen,

my unpainted nail on a word the students see.
I don't upturn callous side. Would they believe. Layers

of deadlifts slathered on my back and thighs.

I photograph how my fibers are tonight
to remind us both that I do exist.

lightyear/eye

I test   *What*
is a lightyear?

        —How old
a light   is in
a year, student jokes.

I think:
light in   a partyhat
        before cake

        but if
it blows
        out, it
blows   out.

A week   after
my birthday I become
committed to contacts again.

It had been
almost a year of only glasses
brow to cheek: in the first

months this felt vulnerable,

clear billboards; I counted other
wearers in the room.

Yet another head
-ache, and I must   relieve my nose.
Unwrap   disks from   moist cocoon,
        silicon-based welcome behind lid.

I really look at my own face for the first time in a year.

Study its age. Stranger
relearned   each time I turn

on the lights these
        next two weeks.

No one says   anything is missing. I side with this.

sally

Is that an armadillo I wonder

about bellyup roaddead
sidelined, until

a second with *No, too*

long. Gator. Texan in Louisiana
must adjust instincts a tad.

Some miles later my car straddles
a turtle's highway pilgrimage.

Not rescuing hurts, but risk burns hotter
on any first lone summer roadtrip.

It's enough to swerve slightly
bringing chicken

jerky and salted corn tortilla chips to mouth.

windows

Returned from jog, you
say some mallard
crossed in front

of you. As if to say *This
is my path, bitch.*

When shown some photos
of bear cubs that piled

into a car with rolled
-down windows,

you say the first
thing you'd worry

about is poop. *Does a bear
shit in the woods* I respond,

as if that axiom chops alternatives.

In my own six-hour car ride to you,
I'm mostly well behaved.

A sip from a large coffee sloshes up
to my right sunglass lens. I lick it off

before considering its cleanliness.

That | thirty | second

On the eve of his birthday 10:00 p.m.
he goes alone to an unnamed film
showing and this happens
over four hundred miles from here,
in a thicker city. I would never
do what he is doing. Why are half the gifts
from his parents possibilities of death:
junk food crisps, day passes for
lessons in pyrotechnics and racecar
driving—and now he applies
a cinema gift card for the latest show time,
and I type *oh ok wow / be safe*.
And I know his brain goes nowhere
near fear. At least not to the alert type I'm thinking.
When we watched movies at the theater
in our twenties and someone grew
old onscreen, he'd cry. Myself, I don't
think of age as foe. Our parents' gifts:
certainties. I want a vastness
between birthday and end.
My circle and his overlapping
in city same.

[o pen in g]

I step on a letter

opener, brass
with handle resembling animal hoof.

The hoof cuts into my bare
foot. I, fool for leaving

such on floor.
I limp alone as sole

occupant in flat.

Red prints in bath
and den.

Among stalagmites
of book piles,

feet socked

and slippered
for better safety.

Tomorrow for the clop
of weightlifting shoes—

more surefooted brute

when my mind
is an envelope left closed.

hartshorn

You don't believe me that smelling
salts are still used.

As if that's just as Victorian

as the girdle my mom
gave me when I turned eleven.

She also thought the sun

might render my leg hair negligible,
never having any herself.

Our armpits are relatable.

On her porch, she and I look
for a lunar eclipse your father says

will happen. My eyelashes tangle

in the cosmos while the stomachs
of deer hold my parents' stalk scraps.

She brings out a jacket she thinks

won't fit my lifter's arms, but it does.
Nothing's changed in the sky. She still

thinks she's bad at physics. Somewhere

nose cones are baking. Somewhere

a woman wafts an ammonia inhalant
before lifting four hundred pounds.

Something whether or not you believe me.

Acknowledgments

Thank you to the editors of the following journals and anthologies for their inclusion of the following poems:

"Brasil & broil" and "Near Igreja de São Domingos, Lisbon": *THRUSH*

"The photoreconnaissance wants an autogiro": *Scrawl Place*

"Render Billow": *FIELD* and *The Literary Review - Share*

"Pages of wrinkled calculus / I suggested for the sun": *SOFTBLOW*

"Supernumerary": *Everything in Aspic*

"unerased | steep steps": *Abandon Journal*

"gestures": *Dialogist*

"ad|mire": *Foundry*

"Spring Lake": *Sublunary Review*

"Piranha Plop": *Monster: A Miracle Monocle Micro-Anthology*

"hartshorn": *I Scream Social Anthology* vol. 2

I would also like to thank the editors and panelists for the following honors while *pH of Au* was in its manuscript phase:

Finalist for the 2020 Burnside Review Press Book Award
Finalist for Lily Poetry Review's 2021 Paul Nemser Book Prize
Semifinalist for the 2021 Switchback Books' Gatewood Prize
Semifinalist for the 2021 The Word Works' Washington Prize
Longlisted for the 2021 Cowles Poetry Book Prize

Much gratitude, muito obrigada, to Jon Thompson and David Blakesley.

About the Author

Vanessa Couto Johnson (she/they) is the author of the full-length prose poetry book *Pungent dins concentric* (Tolsun Books, 2018) and three poetry chapbooks: *Life of Francis* (winner of Gambling the Aisle's 2014 Chapbook Contest), *rotoscoping collage in Cork City* (dancing girl press, 2016), and *speech rinse* (winner of Slope Edition's 2016 Chapbook Contest). Most recently, Vanessa's poems have appeared in *The Collidescope, Star 82 Review, TERSE. Journal,* and *Superstition Review,* and her creative nonfiction appears in *The Account* and *FEED.* A Brazilian who was born in Texas (a dual citizen), VCJ has taught at Texas State University since 2014.

Photograph of the author by Samuel Wilson. Used by permission.

Free Verse Editions

Edited by Jon Thompson

An Unchanging Blue: Selected Poems 1962–1975 by Rolf Dieter
    Brinkmann, trans. by Mark Terrill
Under the Quick by Molly Bendall
Verge by Morgan Lucas Schuldt
The Visible Woman by Allison Funk
The Wash by Adam Clay
We'll See by Georges Godeau, trans. by Kathleen McGookey
What Stillness Illuminated by Yermiyahu Ahron Taub
Winter Journey [Viaggio d'inverno] by Attilio Bertolucci, trans. by
    Nicholas Benson
Wonder Rooms by Allison Funk

www.ingramcontent.com/pod-product-compliance
Lightning Source LLC
Chambersburg PA
CBHW021508090426
42739CB00007B/524